Little Laureates

# Scottish Poets

Edited by Claire Tupholme

YoungWriters
First published in Great Britain in 2007 by:
Young Writers
Remus House
Coltsfoot Drive
Peterborough
PE2 9JX
Telephone: 01733 890066
Website: www.youngwriters.co.uk



SB ISBN 978-1 84431 222 1

# Foreword

Young Writers was established in 1991 and has been passionately devoted to the promotion of reading and writing in children and young adults ever since. The quest continues today. Young Writers remains as committed to the nurturing of poetic and literary talent as ever.

This year's Young Writers competition has proven as vibrant and dynamic as ever and we are delighted to present a showcase of the best poetry from across the UK and in some cases overseas. Each poem has been selected from a wealth of *Little Laureates* entries before ultimately being published in this, our sixteenth primary school poetry series.

Once again, we have been supremely impressed by the overall quality of the entries we have received. The imagination, energy and creativity which has gone into each young writer's entry made choosing the poems a challenging and often difficult but ultimately hugely rewarding task - the general high standard of the work submitted ensured this opportunity to bring their poetry to a larger appreciative audience.

We sincerely hope you are pleased with this final collection and that you will enjoy *Little Laureates Scottish Poets* for many years to come.

# Contents


**Abbotswell Primary School, Aberdeen**

| | |
|---|---|
| Ross Campbell (9) | 1 |
| Greg Davidson (9) | 2 |
| Daniel Dodds (9) | 3 |
| Rachel Gibbons (8) | 4 |
| Annmarie Henderson (9) | 5 |
| Rebecca Innes (8) | 6 |
| Alex McGillivray (9) | 7 |
| Michael McLeary (8) | 8 |
| Samantha McQueen (9) | 9 |
| Dean Menzies (9) | 10 |
| Aiden Newlands (8) | 11 |
| Jade Ogston (8) | 12 |
| Ellie Robertson (8) | 13 |
| Brandon Russell (8) | 14 |
| Chanelle Slessor (8) | 15 |
| Amy Smith (8) | 16 |
| Donald Stewart (8) | 17 |
| Liam Tarburn (8) | 18 |
| Abigail Watt (8) | 19 |
| Callum Watt (8) | 20 |
| Dominic Watt (8) | 21 |
| Megan Wood (8) | 22 |

**Ashley Road School, Aberdeen**

| | |
|---|---|
| Ross Provan (10) | 23 |
| Dale Boardman (10) | 24 |
| Jessica Potts (9) | 25 |
| Louise Walker (10) | 26 |
| Jasmine Hindson (9) | 27 |
| Oscar Stark (9) | 28 |
| Anna Duguid (9) | 29 |
| Samuel Panza Mijares (9) | 30 |
| Andrew McLaren (9) | 31 |
| James Maddox (10) | 32 |
| David McAllan (10) | 33 |
| Daniel McCartney (10) | 34 |
| Susannah Scott (9) | 35 |
| Kelsey Bisset (9) | 36 |

Mitchell Cassie (9) 37
Nicholas Lindsay (10) 38
Stephen McIntosh (9) 39
Callie McPherson (9) 40
Alex Morrison (10) 41
Rob Muir (10) 42
Jack Lovie (10) 43

**Baird Memorial Primary School, Cumbernauld**
Greg Dearle (7) 44
Darren Ingram (7) 45
Adam Dempsey (7) 46
Rebecca Harvey (7) 47
Andrew Michie (8) 48

**Beauly Primary School, Beauly**
Grant Wilson (10) 49
Charlotte Wilde (10) 50
Katie Stephen-McAllister (11) 51
Emma Ross (9) 52
Emma MacKenzie (9) 53
James Marshall (10) 54
Cameron McDonald (9) 55
Colin MacDonald (11) 56
Graeme Lashley (10) 57
Caitlin MacDonald (9) 58
Beth MacDonald (11) 59
Rob Hardie (11) 60
Kirsty Fraser (10) 61
Sara Di Carlo (10) 62
Georgia Coleman (9) 63
Natasha Campbell (10) 64
Rebecca Weston (10) 65
Rebecca Moss (11) 66
James Cameron (9) 67
Jordan Bradshaw (11) 68

**Burgh Primary School, Galashiels**
Zennor Bacon, Danielle Doogan
& Dominka Jagielska (9) 69
Ben Gill (9) 70

Jack Halls & Andrew Bennett (9) 71
Liam Nicholson & Aidan Turner (9) 72
Wiktor Hyzy (10) & Greg Rathie (9) 73
Paulina Imbiorkiewicz & Hannah Maben (9) 74
Parris Murray (10) & Alihya Aziz (9) 75
Fraser Brown & Jay Allan (9) 76

**Crathes Primary School, Crathes**
Jenny Lusby (8) 77
Garran Sutton (11) 78
Cameron Booth (10) 79

**Dunnottar Primary School, Stonehaven**
Jessie Knowles (9) 80
Rachael Bonds (9) 81
Lucy Kennedy (8) 82
Oscar Craig (8) 83
Stuart Holley (9) 84
Matthew Ogden (8) 85

**Fallin Primary School, Fallin**
Steven Macleod (10) 86
Billy Irvine (10) 87
Blair Maxwell (10) 88
Conor Paterson (10) 89
Erin Perrie (10) 90
Ross McTaggart (10) 91
Liam Kirkwood (10) 92
Lauren Smith (10) 93
Taylor Reid (10) 94
Cheryl Rooney (10) 95
Natalie Gow (8) 96
Karlee Manson (9) 97
Leigh Young (9) 98
Alex Govan (9) 99
Lisa Brennan (10) 100

**Johnshaven Primary School, Johnshaven**
Holly Chandler (10) 101
Grant Keith (11) 102

Laura Townsend (9) 103
Miranda-Beth Leavens (9) 104
Holly Marwick (10) 105
Lauren Anderson (10) 106
Lewis Pollock (10) 107
Lisa Porter (7) 108
Kathryn Townsend (6) 109
Hamish Wright (8) 110
Dillon Scott (8) 111
Kyle Boyd (8) 112
Rhys Gardiner (11) 113
Murray Dunbar (9) 114
Stephanie Brannan 115
Tiele Brannan (10) 116

**Juniper Green Primary School, Edinburgh**
Claire McNicoll (11) 117
Megan Mackay (10) 118
Katie Hill (11) 119
Bonnie Fisher (10) 120
Murray Drummond (10) 121
Shaun Munro (11) 122
Emma Newlands (10) 123

**Kennethmont School, Huntly**
Erin Allan (11) 124
Daniel Coursey (9) 125
Peter Duthie (11) 126
Kyle Florence (10) 127
Angus MacLean (11) 128
Morgan McCallum (11) 129
Matthew Robertson (10) 130
Cara Simpson (11) 131
Rebekah Watson (10) 132

**Kirkmichael Primary School, Blairgowrie**
Stephanie Curtis (11) 133
Fiona Van Der Veldt (11) 134
Aarron Laidler (10) 135
Holly Brown (10) 136
Frankie Moore (10) 137

Claire Van Der Veldt (10) 138
Annie Winton (11) 139

**Knoxland Primary School, Dumbarton**
Ross Ferguson (12) 140
Alexander Brown (12) 141
Jordan Brooks (11) 142
Mark Provan (11) 143
Liam Troup (12) 144
Isla Neil (12) 145
Ashlinn Weber (11) 146
Laura Fleming (12) 147
Rebecca Bell (11) 148
Stephen Bennett (11) 149
Sean Deeney (11) 150
Jenna Wilson (11) 151
Gemma Kitchen (11) 152
Becky Fisher (11) 153
Scott Dallas (11) 154
Jordan MacLean (11) 155
Calum Harper (11) 156
Scott Connie (12) 157
Gillian McElroy (12) 158
Stacey O'Hara (12) 159
Ruaraidh MacGregor (11) 160
Andrew McKenzie (12) 161
Rebecca Law (11) 162
Graeme Burt (11) 163
Kirsty Harrison (12) 164
Konal Lee (11) 165
Craig Runciman (12) 166
Shannon Smith (12) 167
Jade Smith (11) 168
Scott Major (11) 169
David McCaffary (11) 170
Jordan Ferguson (12) 171
Rebecca Lyall (12) 172
Callum MacLeod (11) 173
Calum Donaghy (11) 174
Iain Allen (11) 175

**Longforgan Primary School, Longforgan**

Chloe Randall (8) 176
Holly Hutchison (7) 177
Beth McNeish (7) 178
Robyn McNally (7) 179
Lucy Stewart (8) 180
Ryan Anderson (8) 181
Kieran Fitzgerald (8) 182
Ryan Lonie (8) 183
Heather Morgans (8) 184
Bruce Kerr (8) 185
Lauren Hutton (9) 186
Murray Macdonald (8) 187
Rebecca Strachan (8) 188

**Wardie Primary School, Edinburgh**

Tori Grigg (9) 189
Samantha Fyfe (9) 190
Paul Macrae (10) 191
Joe Newman (9) 192
James Tait (9) 193
Rory McDermid (10) 194
Kaitlin Maloney (9) 195
Ryan Crombie (10) 196
Lynsey Wilson (9) 197
Ben Paterson (9) 198
Evan Adair (10) 199
Caitriona Campbell (10) & Justyna Kazmeerzack (11) 200
Morgan Ormiston (9) 201
Andrew Gray (10) 202
Mia Harley (9) 203

# The Poems

## Happiness Is . . .

Happiness is bright yellow
It tastes like smooth custard in my mouth
And smells like a hot pancake
It looks like the blazing sun in the clear blue sky
And sounds like beautiful birds tweeting in the trees
Happiness is playing on the green grass

Happiness is great!

**Ross Campbell (9)**
**Abbotswell Primary School, Aberdeen**

## It!

It was horrifying.
It was rotten.
It jumped out of the TV screen.

It was gigantic.
It was huge.
It had a million bulging eyes.

It was frightening.
It was slimy.
It had teeth as sharp as a razor.

It was fierce.
It was revolting.
It had horrible stinking breath.

It was hideous.
It was ugly.
It vanished.
That was *it!*

**Greg Davidson (9)**
**Abbotswell Primary School, Aberdeen**

# It

It was rotten.
It was gross.
It came shooting out of my toilet.

It was spiky.
It was spotty.
It had two bulging heads.

It was muddy.
It was angry.
It had smelly sharp teeth.

It was green and slimy.
It was disgusting.
It had six dirty arms.

It was slim
It was hairy.

It vanished . . .
That was *it!*

**Daniel Dodds (9)**
**Abbotswell Primary School, Aberdeen**

# It

It was horrifying.
It was revolting.
It jumped out of my toy box.

It was scaly.
It was lazy.
It had green webbed feet like a frog.

It was gigantic.
It was lazy.
It had ten red eyes that looked evil.

It was angry.
It was moody.
It had twenty teeth as sharp as razors.

It was dirty.
It was sticky.

It vanished . . .
That was *it!*

**Rachel Gibbons (8)**
**Abbotswell Primary School, Aberdeen**

## Happiness Is . . .

Happiness is light lilac.
It tastes like a slice of Mum's tasty fruit cake
And smells like fresh, sweet roses.
It looks like a fiery sunset reflecting the sea
And sounds like dolphins echoing in the distance.
Happiness is feeling my grandma tickling my back.
Happiness is terrific!

**Annmarie Henderson (9)**
**Abbotswell Primary School, Aberdeen**

## A Recipe For Winter

Take a mug of steaming hot chocolate
Some dancing snowflakes swirling in the sky
And a sheet of smooth, shiny ice.

Stir in a roasting coal fire
A robin redbreast perched on an icy branch
And a big gust of whistling wind.

Decorate with wreaths on front doors
Some cosy hats, scarves and gloves
And carol singers at my door.

Leave in the freezer for three long months
Now you have made winter!

**Rebecca Innes (8)**
**Abbotswell Primary School, Aberdeen**

## Happiness Is . . .

Happiness is bright orange.
It tastes like hundreds and thousands sitting on a doughnut
And smells like my grandad's home-made toffee on Sunday evening.
It looks like the views out of my auntie's kitchen window
And sounds like my fluffy cat purring softly on my bed.
Happiness is the bubbles around me in the bath.
Happiness is fun!

**Alex McGillivray (9)**
**Abbotswell Primary School, Aberdeen**

## Happiness Is . . .

Happiness is sparkling gold.
It tastes like lots of melted chocolate sensations
And smells like delicious toffee popcorn.
It looks like the shiny sun in the clear blue sky
And sounds like popcorn crackling in the microwave.
Happiness is feeling my cosy blanket.
Happiness is sweet!

**Michael McLeary (8)**
**Abbotswell Primary School, Aberdeen**

## It!

It was ugly.
It was spotty.
It jumped out from under my bed.

It was gigantic.
It was fat.
It had ten red, glowing eyes.

It was smelly.
It was scary.
It had big, sharp, rotten teeth.

It was strong.
It was vicious.
It had a long, big, spiky tail.

It was fierce.
It was disgusting.

It vanished . . .
That was *it!*

**Samantha McQueen (9)**
**Abbotswell Primary School, Aberdeen**

## A Recipe For Winter

Take some shiny smooth ice,
A big, huge gust of wind
And a cup of hot chocolate.

Mix with a big white snowman,
Children flying down hills on their sledges
And snowflakes like light feathers in the sky.

Cover with chocolate spread on hot toast,
A pair of gloves and a hat
And a lovely hot fire.

Leave in the freezer for three long months.
Now you have made winter!

**Dean Menzies (9)**
**Abbotswell Primary School, Aberdeen**

## It

It was rotten.
It was ferocious.
It came shooting out of my toilet.

It was smelly.
It was huge.
It had four red eyes like golf balls.

It was strong.
It was slim.
It had a huge, runny nose that dripped everywhere.

It was dirty.
It was stinky.
It had sharp teeth that hung right down.

It was revolting.
It was scary.

It vanished . . .
That was *it!*

**Aiden Newlands (8)**
**Abbotswell Primary School, Aberdeen**

## Happiness Is . . .

Happiness is pure gold.
It tastes like chocolate melting on squishy marshmallows in a bowl
And smells like beautiful perfume that's made from red roses.
It looks like cuddly puppies sleeping in a basket
And sounds like an orchestra playing romantic music.
Happiness is feeling the warm breeze on my face when I walk.
Happiness is wonderful!

**Jade Ogston (8)**
**Abbotswell Primary School, Aberdeen**

## Happiness Is . . .

Happiness is bright pink.
It tastes like sweet and sour smoothies
And smells like my strawberry perfume.
It looks like Christmas lights in the dark night sky
And sounds like bells ringing in the church.
Happiness is feeling a nice hug from my parents.
Happiness is great!

**Ellie Robertson (8)**
**Abbotswell Primary School, Aberdeen**

## Happiness Is . . .

Happiness is light blue.
It tastes like a pizza smothered in melting cheese
And smells like sweet candyfloss from the funfair.
It looks like a baby sleeping in a red pram
And sounds like bees buzzing as they land to get pollen.
Happiness is feeling my dog's slobbery kisses.
Happiness is perfect!

**Brandon Russell (8)**
**Abbotswell Primary School, Aberdeen**

## A Recipe For Winter

Take some dancing, icy snowflakes from the sky,
A robin redbreast perched on a tall, high tree
And a lonely snowman in a long, white garden.

Add a steaming mug of hot chocolate,
Carol singers at your door
And children wearing hats and scarves in the snow.

Cover with roast turkey and all the lovely trimmings,
A child opening Santa's presents
And lights outside my door twinkling.

Leave it in the freezer for three long months.
Now you have made winter!

**Chanelle Slessor (8)**
**Abbotswell Primary School, Aberdeen**

## A Recipe For Winter

Take a nice cup of steaming hot chocolate
A fierce gust of wind
And beautiful, dancing snowflakes.

Add some delicious turkey
Some freezing, sparkling ice
And some exciting snowball fights.

Decorate with freezing icicles
A snow angel
And a robin redbreast on a sparkling tree.

Leave in the freezer for three long months
Now you have made winter!

**Amy Smith (8)**
**Abbotswell Primary School, Aberdeen**

## Happiness Is . . .

Happiness is blistering red.
It tastes like melting custard and chocolate in my mouth
And smells like syrup in a hot pancake.
It looks like a roasting ball of fire
And sounds like fire crackling in the woods.
Happiness is swimming in the swimming pool with my friend.
Happiness is brilliant!

**Donald Stewart (8)**
**Abbotswell Primary School, Aberdeen**

## Happiness Is . . .

Happiness is sparkling blue.
It tastes like a warm bowl of golden custard
And smells like a bit of my mum's carrot cake.
It looks like the city view set right in front of you
And sounds like the dolphins echoing at the beach.
Happiness is feeling nice thoughts deep down inside.
Happiness is unbelievable!

**Liam Tarburn (8)**
**Abbotswell Primary School, Aberdeen**

## A Recipe For Winter

Take some dancing snowflakes from the sky
Some shining and sparkling white snow
And a beautiful white snowman.

Stir in dancing snow angels
Some twinkling, beautiful stars
And sparkling icicles hanging from the roof.

Sprinkle with fluffy snow under my feet
Some twinkling lights
And woolly gloves and hats.

Leave in the freezer for three long months.
Now you have made winter!

**Abigail Watt (8)**
**Abbotswell Primary School, Aberdeen**

# It

It was smelly.
It was hideous.
It came flying out of the loo.

It was lazy.
It was ugly.
It had a razor-sharp horn on its forehead.

It was bony.
It was goofy.
It had one bulging eye.

It was humungous.
It was strong.
It had a weird haircut.

It was revolting.
It was angry.

It vanished . . .
That was *it!*

**Callum Watt (8)**
**Abbotswell Primary School, Aberdeen**

## Happiness Is . . .

Happiness is light green.
It tastes like slimy, melting chocolate doughnuts
And smells like aftershave floating through the air.
It looks like baby rabbits
And sounds like a rock band.
Happiness is feeling Daniel tickle me.
Happiness is life!

**Dominic Watt (8)**
**Abbotswell Primary School, Aberdeen**

# It

It was fierce.
It was revolting.
It emerged from under the floorboards.

It was spiky.
It was smelly.
It had a gigantic tail like a scorpion.

It was lazy.
It was gross.
It had a big orange eye, the shape of a ball.

It was wrinkly.
It was fat.
It had huge floppy ears like a rabbit.

It was tall.
It was dirty.

It vanished . . .
That was *it!*

**Megan Wood (8)**
**Abbotswell Primary School, Aberdeen**

## In The Rainforest

I can smell the roaring scent of a flower.
I can hear the toucan's song that beats for an hour.
I can taste a stream of coconut milk from the trees.
I can feel the wet snakes hanging in the breeze.
I can see the beautiful sight of the fun that makes it look honest.
I can see jaguars in a tropical rainforest.

**Ross Provan (10)**
**Ashley Road School, Aberdeen**

## In The Rainforest

I can touch the smooth, damp, green skin of a South American
tree frog.
I can see the brown, dead, crispy leaves that have fallen from
a tree to their doom.
I can hear the ear-piercing roar of a jaguar as it kills its prey.
I can smell the luxurious scent of the beautiful flowers of
the rainforest.
I can taste the invigorating juice of a mango and the weak skin
of a cherry.

**Dale Boardman (10)**
**Ashley Road School, Aberdeen**

## In The Rainforest

I can feel the rough bark of the terrific trees.
I can see the candyfloss clouds in the beautiful blue sky.
I can hear the rain going *pitter-patter, pitter-patter.*
I can taste the juicy, yummy fruit in the terrific trees.
I can smell the scent of the fantastic flowers.

**Jessica Potts (9)**
**Ashley Road School, Aberdeen**

## In The Rainforest

In the rainforest I can feel the rough, long, old bark of the
rainforest trees.
In the rainforest I can see the Bengal tiger jump 5 metres in the
rainforest's warm summer air.
In the rainforest I can hear the early morning birds making the song
of the morning.
In the rainforest I can smell the familiar scent of the big, huge,
giant panda at the side of the river.
In the rainforest you can taste big, juicy, mouth-watering pineapple
from the tall, huge, giant, green trees.

**Louise Walker (10)**
**Ashley Road School, Aberdeen**

## In A Rainforest

I can see the fierce looking jaguar going to attack its prey.
I can hear the old, tall, hard tree leaves shivering from the
wind's power.
I can smell the wonderfully magical flowers showing off their scents.
I can taste the sweetness of the oranges with a juicy centre.
I can touch the skimming, relaxing water from the silvery stream.

**Jasmine Hindson (9)**
**Ashley Road School, Aberdeen**

## In The Rainforest

I can see the dark, gloomy bark on the rainforest floor,
Where everything is incredibly dark.
I can touch the damp fallen leaves in the rainforest,
Where they fall from the trees.
I can hear the eerie, creaking noise whistling in the breeze,
In and out and about all of the trees.
I can taste the dry bread, foul to the mouth
And hurtful to the head.
I can smell the stench of the rotting leaves, the horrible smell
Makes it hard to believe that they were once part of the elegant trees.

**Oscar Stark (9)**
**Ashley Road School, Aberdeen**

## In The Rainforest

I can touch the damp, rigid, tough green and brown trees.
I can see the river floating and shimmering through the waterfall as
it passes the trees.
I can hear the big bright birds singing in the sky.
I can smell a scent of pollen as a butterfly passes me, flying with
bright, cheerful wings into the clouds.
I can taste the fresh, juicy fruit running down my throat.

**Anna Duguid (9)**
**Ashley Road School, Aberdeen**

## In The Rainforest

I can see the rainforest as miles and miles of green-brown, tall
Oak, beech, elm, pine and many more short, wide and crispy trees.
I can feel the big, round, hairy and brown, good-looking,
Hard coconut.
I can hear the cunning snakes slithering and the mighty lion
Roaring loudly in the undergrowth.
I can taste the succulent berries and the ripe, juicy mango.
I can smell the spectacular scent of the beautiful, brightly-coloured
flowers.

**Samuel Panza Mijares (9)**
**Ashley Road School, Aberdeen**

## In The Rainforest

I can touch the prickly leaves on top of the silky smooth grass
With tiny pieces of ridged wood from trees,
On the ground of the rainforest.

I can see the huge trees tumbling down for paper
And see an amazing spider making a white, silky web.

I can hear the animals fighting with their sharp claws
And shouting very loudly at each other over something.

I can smell the lovely trees and flowers
In the rainforest of the Amazon.

I can taste amazing apples on the shiny ground
And the oranges on the tiny trees.

**Andrew McLaren (9)**
**Ashley Road School, Aberdeen**

## In The Rainforest

I can touch the smooth, soft, warm, thick fur of the jaguar.
I can see the huge, harpy eagle swooping and diving
Through the trees, chasing her prey.
I can hear the song of the howler monkey screaming in the trees.
I can smell the wafting smells of the different exotic plants.
I can taste the sweet, juicy, succulent, big, wild and exotic
Fruit from the trees.

**James Maddox (10)**
**Ashley Road School, Aberdeen**

## In The Rainforest

I can touch the hard, crunching texture of the trees.
I can hear the great howl of the wolf as it wanders through
The dark, gloomy night.
I can see the sly-witted jaguar crunching through
The brown, crinkled leaves.
I can smell the haunting aroma of the beautiful budding tulips.
I can taste the sweet, juicy, squishy berries from the autumn bushes.

**David McAllan (10)**
**Ashley Road School, Aberdeen**

## In the Rainforest

I can touch the soft, hairy bark on the sides of the trees.
I can see the big, fat crocodile sitting on the riverbank,
Waiting for an animal to walk past.
I can hear a monkey's loud shout to its friends.
I can smell the scent of damp grass sitting on the ground.
I can taste the damp, wet air floating around me.

**Daniel McCartney (10)**
**Ashley Road School, Aberdeen**

## In The Rainforest

I can see the toucan's huge, magnificent, colourful beak.
I can smell the huge, beautiful flowers sprouting up all around me.
I can touch the small, green, spiky bushes on the forest floor.
I can taste all the wonderful fruits that have very juicy flavours.
I can hear the big, sly tiger hunting its prey in the long grass.

**Susannah Scott (9)**
**Ashley Road School, Aberdeen**

## In The Rainforest

I can taste the sweet, creamy coconut milk,
Freshly picked from a coconut.
I can touch the rough bronze bark,
That has fallen gently from the tall trees.
I can see a tiger ready for its prey,
With fear in its shiny, green, round eyes.
I can smell the juicy, fair, yellow melons,
Hanging from the trees.
I can hear the solo song of colourful,
Eye-catching, noisy birds.

**Kelsey Bisset (9)**
**Ashley Road School, Aberdeen**

## In The Rainforest

I can see a jaguar pounding and birds bouncing.
I can hear monkeys swinging and branches breaking.
I can smell the deadly scent of poisonous plants.
I can touch the hard oak tree wood
And I can taste bugs flying into my mouth.

**Mitchell Cassie (9)**
**Ashley Road School, Aberdeen**

## In The Rainforest

In the rainforest I can smell the beautiful scent of the golden
lavender herb.
In the rainforest I can taste the unique flavour of a banana
fresh from a tree.
In the rainforest I can hear the amazing macaw
humming an amazing song.
In the rainforest I can feel the hard, cold rain
beating on my body.
In the rainforest I can see the amazing tiger,
jumping at its unlucky prey.

**Nicholas Lindsay (10)**
**Ashley Road School, Aberdeen**

## In The Rainforest

I can touch the non poisonous animals with good kind senses.
I can taste the lovely round coconuts tumbling down from the trees.
I can smell the dumped, dead animals with red blood and mud
over them.
I can hear the snakes sliding through the grubby, filthy grass and
hissing as they go.
I can see the soft, furry jaguars with brill skills up and down trees.

**Stephen McIntosh (9)**
**Ashley Road School, Aberdeen**

## In The Rainforest

I can feel the smooth, waxy skin of a manatee.
I can see beautiful colours from the forest plants.
I can hear the screeching of monkeys high up in the trees.
I can smell the sweet scent of honey from the killer bees.
I can taste the sweet, luscious fruit of the forest.

**Callie McPherson (9)**
**Ashley Road School, Aberdeen**

## In The Rainforest

I can hear the harpy eagle chicks chirping for their food
And the squirrel monkeys falling through the branches.

I can hear the piranhas devouring the fishes' skin
In the murky Amazon river.

I can see the slow sloth
Make contact with the ground.

I can feel the wet, slimy trunks of a tapir as it drools over my hand
And the short, hairy coat of the ocelot.

I can taste the nice fruitful taste of the banana
High up in the trees.

I can smell the fresh air and the horrible smell of the sloth
Which smells appalling.

**Alex Morrison (10)**
**Ashley Road School, Aberdeen**

## In The Rainforest

I can see swinging Tarsiers flying through the trees like Tarzan.
I can hear a Siberian tiger prowling round its young, crunching the
dead leaves.
I can touch the rough damp bark of a tree.
I can smell the disgusting smell of jaguar manure.
I can taste the milk from a coconut that has fallen from a tree.

**Rob Muir (10)**
**Ashley Road School, Aberdeen**

## Rainforest

I can taste the tropical scent of the trees
I can touch the damp leaves that have been bitten by the caterpillar
I can hear the slippery snakes as they slither through damp leaves
I can smell the very rough trees' dampness
I can see the squirrels jumping off the trees one by one.

**Jack Lovie (10)**
**Ashley Road School, Aberdeen**

## My Dog

I have a dog
He is so small
He curls in a ball.

He is small, not tall
He is such fun
We play in the sun.

**Greg Dearle (7)**
**Baird Memorial Primary School, Cumbernauld**

## Reptiles Poem

A snake is long
A tortoise is fat
It's got a big shell
On its back.

A dragon is big
A lizard is small
It has jaggy bits
On its back.

**Darren Ingram (7)**
**Baird Memorial Primary School, Cumbernauld**

## My Friends

I like my friends.
They are fun.
We go to the grassy.
It is fun.
I like my friends.
They are great.
We go to the wall until eight.

I like my friends.
They are cool.
We go to the swimming baths
To play in the pool.

**Adam Dempsey (7)**
**Baird Memorial Primary School, Cumbernauld**

## My Dog

My dog is rough,
My dog is tough,
My dog is furry,
He likes Rachel Murray.

He barks and barks
And never stops.
He will not watch
'Top of the Pops'.

He is white and black
And has blue eyes.
When it's time for his walk,
He gets a big surprise.

**Rebecca Harvey (7)**
**Baird Memorial Primary School, Cumbernauld**

## I Like My Brother

I like my brother,
He is fun,
As fun as fun can be.

We play football
And he is the goalie.
I let him win
Because he is my kin.

I like my brother.

**Andrew Michie (8)**
**Baird Memorial Primary School, Cumbernauld**

## Hate

Hate is red, like blood on a sword.
It smells like a gloomy, dark morgue.
Hate looks like a lonely corner in a dark room.
Hate feels like lightning down your back in a thunderstorm led
by the Devil.
It reminds me of spikes, flames and Satan himself.
Hate sounds like a violent rage and a pounding heart.
It tastes like a blood-smothered chicken, killed fresh from the farm.

**Grant Wilson (10)**
**Beauly Primary School, Beauly**

## Death

Death is black, like the bottom of the ocean.
It smells like rotten air.
Death feels like you're drowning in the sea.
It sounds like footsteps behind you, but no one is there.
Death tastes like a rotten apple left in an abandoned room.
It looks like a ghost ready to kill.
Death reminds me of being alone in a graveyard at midnight.

**Charlotte Wilde (10)**
**Beauly Primary School, Beauly**

## Happiness

Happiness is yellow, like sunshine
Happiness reminds me of seeing my family and friends
Happiness feels good because you're having a good time
Happiness tastes like ice cream on a hot, sunny day
Happiness smells like roses in a garden
Happiness looks like fun and playing all around
Happiness sounds like kids having a great time.

**Katie Stephen-McAllister (11)**
**Beauly Primary School, Beauly**

## My Two Cats

My two cats are very cute,
One's called Mika and the other's called Blue.
If you think they're both alike,
Well, you are definitely not right.
Blue is fat, Mika is thin,
One jumps into a heap of fastening pins.
One destroys newspapers that are left on the floor,
The other goes and headbuts the sitting room door.
The only time they're quiet again
Is when they're fast asleep in their beds!

**Emma Ross (9)**
**Beauly Primary School, Beauly**

## Secret Garden

Thorny, wild flowers
All different bright colours
Stream rushing down and all around
A pond full of goldfish
A kitten licking from a milk dish
Fairies flying across the stream
Air getting hot by the sunbeam
A child rolling through piles of leaves
A gateway covered by ivy.

**Emma MacKenzie (9)**
**Beauly Primary School, Beauly**

## Courage

Courage reminds me of glory and honour.
Courage feels like water trickling down your spine.
It sounds like swords clashing in a great battle.
Courage looks like a medal of honour.
Courage is orange, just like the giant sun.
Courage tastes like a gulp of bravery.

**James Marshall (10)**
**Beauly Primary School, Beauly**

## Fear

Fear is black, like the night sky
It tastes like heartburn in my gut
It smells like the cold night air
It reminds me of ghostly ghouls
Fear feels like my body tingling and screaming
It sounds like ghastly groans and moans.

**Cameron McDonald (9)**
**Beauly Primary School, Beauly**

## Hate

Hate is red, like the fires of Hell.
Hate sounds like people shouting and screaming.
Hate tastes like slimy Brussels sprouts in the pit of your stomach.
Hate smells like burning wood rotting away in a fire.
Hate looks like the gates of Hell.
Hate feels like a fireball in your throat.
Hate reminds me of the Devil.

**Colin MacDonald (11)**
**Beauly Primary School, Beauly**

## Flowers - Cinquain

Flowers
Pretty colours
Daffodil and daisy
Pollen and bees zooming around
Garden!

**Graeme Lashley (10)**
**Beauly Primary School, Beauly**

## Darkness

Darkness is like
The navy blue sky

Darkness looks like
Grey clouds moving in the sky

Darkness reminds me
Of when my grandad died

Darkness feels like
You're in a really small box, dark and empty

Darkness sounds like
Complete silence

Darkness tastes like
Air going down your throat, making you feel cold and sad.

**Caitlin MacDonald (9)**
**Beauly Primary School, Beauly**

# Fun

Fun is yellow, like the sweet sunshine.
Fun smells like burning sausages on the barbecue.
Fun reminds me of children playing.
Fun tastes like melting chocolate on a hot day.
Fun feels like I can do anything I want.
Fun sounds like everyone enjoying themselves.

**Beth MacDonald (11)**
**Beauly Primary School, Beauly**

## My Dog

My dog is gold, like the yellow of a burning fire.
He feels like a soft fur coat.
He sounds like a wolf crying at midnight.
He looks like a bushy, fluffy tail.
He reminds me of all the good things in life, like chocolate and Coke.
He smells like a vase of freshly cut flowers.

**Rob Hardie (11)**
**Beauly Primary School, Beauly**

## Love!

Love is red, like a heart never to be broken.
It smells like a thousand roses in the sweet spring air.
Love tastes like melting chocolate on a hot summer's day.
Love looks like a happy couple holding hands as they walk
into the sunset.
It sounds like laughter when people are enjoying themselves.
Love feels like a soft kiss upon your cheek.
Love reminds me of roses swaying in the wind.

**Kirsty Fraser (10)**
**Beauly Primary School, Beauly**

## Sheep

Sheep are white with a curly coat,
They went in two by two on Noah's boat.
Everyone knows that sheep are daft,
They would follow each other onto a raft.
When sheep have babies, they are called lambs,
And other sheep are called rams.
Sheep live on farms, sometimes in barns,
I know sheep wouldn't eat your arms.
Sheep and rams like to eat grass,
Out of their mouths, they release gas.
At the end of the day,
They go away,
To get some rest,
It's for the best,
To prepare for a brand new day.

**Sara Di Carlo (10)**
**Beauly Primary School, Beauly**

## Ploda Falls

Ploda smells like delicate roses
Ploda tastes like tangy, sweet berries leaving a sensation
In your mouth
Sounds like a great amount of water rushing to the beach
Ploda looks like Heaven, a dream come true
Ploda is white, like heavenly clouds dancing in the sky
Ploda feels like flying with angels
Reminds me of my grandfather who is as great as Ploda.

**Georgia Coleman (9)**
**Beauly Primary School, Beauly**

## A Baby

A baby's skin is peach, like a juicy apricot
A baby smells like a pot of cream, fresh from the dairy
A baby sounds like a soft cry echoing through the woods
A baby tastes like a sweet sensation in your mouth
A baby looks like a tender cloud floating in the sky
A baby feels like a piece of Heaven drifting down into your dreams
A baby reminds me of youth, a new beginning.

**Natasha Campbell (10)**
**Beauly Primary School, Beauly**

## Sadness

Sadness is blue, like the Dead Sea
It feels like a knife through your heart
Sounds like someone told me someone's just died
Sadness looks all blurry because of the tears running down my face
It reminds me of bad things that have happened to me
It tastes like salty tears
Sadness smells like an airless room.

**Rebecca Weston (10)**
**Beauly Primary School, Beauly**

## Sadness

Sadness feels like a knot tied in your throat
When you don't want to cry.
Sadness sounds like a crying family
When they have been told something bad.
It tastes like cold air going down your throat
Just waiting to make you choke.
Sadness is a dull blue
Like Heaven crying on a stormy night.
Sadness reminds me of when
I was told my gran died.

**Rebecca Moss (11)**
**Beauly Primary School, Beauly**

## Fun

Fun is yellow, like sunshine on a sunny day
It sounds like people enjoying themselves
It looks like the funfair with people shouting
It reminds me of my first day out at the shows
Fun tastes like candyfloss, sweet and sticky
It smells like good food that you get everywhere
It feels like I am tired, I've had a good day!

**James Cameron (9)**
**Beauly Primary School, Beauly**

# Hate

Hate is red like cells in your blood.
Hate tastes like sour milk.
Hate feels like sadness and loneliness.
Hate sounds like a thousand glass bottles smashed on the ground.
Hate looks like your best friend will not be your friend anymore.
Hate reminds me of the Devil inside me.
Hate smells like a skunk making the air smell rotten.

**Jordan Bradshaw (11)**
**Beauly Primary School, Beauly**

## A Spring Tree

Blossom becoming pinker
Leaves looking greener
Branches swaying stronger
Trunk rising higher
Roots spreading longer.

**Zennor Bacon, Danielle Doogan & Dominka Jagielska (9)**
**Burgh Primary School, Galashiels**

## The Scottish Thistle

Scottish flower
Packed together
Prickly grower
Bright stinger
Green jagger.

**Ben Gill (9)**
**Burgh Primary School, Galashiels**

## The Dandelion

Radiant standing petals
Pollen collecting insects
Green dazzling stem
Bumpy crackling veins
Chestnut soft anther
Splendid luminous dandelion.

**Jack Halls & Andrew Bennett (9)**
**Burgh Primary School, Galashiels**

## Cactus

Spiky, prickly spikes
Large, bumpy plant
Strong, flowing roots
Hairy, smelly compost
Green, growing cactus.

**Liam Nicholson & Aidan Turner (9)**
**Burgh Primary School, Galashiels**

## The Biggest Flower

Flowers are pretty and they smell nice
Flowers are showy and bright
Flowers are blossoming and vibrant
Flowers are exotic and interesting
Flowers are colourful and growing.

**Wiktor Hyzy (10) & Greg Rathie (9)**
**Burgh Primary School, Galashiels**

## Sunflowers

Pretty petals blossom
Short leaves blowing
Long stem shooting
Enormous root spindly.

**Paulina Imbiorkiewicz & Hannah Maben (9)**
**Burgh Primary School, Galashiels**

## Roses

Roses are cool
Roses are beautiful
Roses are red
Stems are brown
Stems are thorny
Stems are thin
Leaves are smooth
Leaves are big
Leaves are green.

**Parris Murray (10) & Alihya Aziz (9)**
**Burgh Primary School, Galashiels**

## Cacti Can

Cacti can sting
Cacti can be hurtful
Cacti can prickle
Cacti can protect.

**Fraser Brown & Jay Allan (9)**
**Burgh Primary School, Galashiels**

## The Writer Of This Poem

*(Based on 'The Writer Of This Poem' by Roger McGough)*

The writer of this poem is as thin
As thin can be,
She can be as cold as snow
And as hot as Mercury.

As good as God
And as busy as a bee,
As cool as anyone
At all can be.

The writer of this poem
Is as smart as a fox,
As keen as a soldier
And as pretty as Goldilocks.

As tempting as chocolate
As creamy as a bun,
Good at gymnastics
And never outdone!

**Jenny Lusby (8)**
**Crathes Primary School, Crathes**

## The Writer Of This Poem

*(Based on 'The Writer Of This Poem' by Roger McGough)*

*The writer of this poem*

Is as bright as the sun
As careful as a watchmaker
And likes to get things done

As keen as a leopard
As strong as an ox
As busy as a bee
And as sly as a fox

He's as cautious as a tiger
More angry than a bull
He's as fierce as a cat
But only when he is not at school

He can climb like a monkey
Throw acorns from the tree
Then look out on the ocean
To see the rolling sea

He's wiser than your grandpa
Is harder than a diamond
He can sail like Horatio Nelson
Over to a western island

Not as silent as can be
He's as noisy as a drum
He can roar like a lion
But is quiet when he hums.

**Garran Sutton (11)**
**Crathes Primary School, Crathes**

## The Writer Of This Poem

*(Based on 'The Writer Of This Poem' by Roger McGough)*

The writer of this poem
Is as sharp as knives
Is as good as God's Word
Who lights up everybody's lives

As brilliant as Earth's life
As lovely as light
As handsome as Prince Charming
And stronger than a wolf's bite

As strong as a wrestler
As smart as a mastermind
As keen as an archer
All in all, he's just the best kind

The writer of this poem
Is as clear as days
He's one in a million billion
(Or so the poem says)!

**Cameron Booth (10)**
**Crathes Primary School, Crathes**

## Joy

Joy is turquoise green,
The taste of bright red apples.
Joy is the smell of sweet, pink roses
And an amber, orange sunset.
It sounds like the sweet songs of birds,
Joy is full of happiness!

**Jessie Knowles (9)**
**Dunnottar Primary School, Stonehaven**

## Excuses

I'm sorry I'm late for school, Miss,
But my mum and dad slept in.
I'm sorry I'm late for school, Miss,
But my gran said I'm too thin.
I'm sorry I'm late for school, Miss,
Aliens invaded my house!
I'm sorry I'm late for school, Miss,
My cat choked on a mouse.
I'm sorry I'm late for school, Miss,
But they were handing out chocolate free.
I'm sorry I'm late for school, Miss,
My other cat got stuck up a tree.
I'm sorry I'm late for school, Miss,
But you've really got to believe me,
No, hold on there, please, just you wait and see!

**Rachael Bonds (9)**
**Dunnottar Primary School, Stonehaven**

## Excuses

I'm sorry I'm late for school, Miss,
But I was sick in the car.
I'm sorry I'm late for school, Miss,
But there was lots of haar.
I'm sorry I'm late for school, Miss,
My cat got stuck up a tree.
I'm sorry I'm late for school, Miss,
There was a shop giving out things for free!
I'm sorry I'm late for school, Miss,
But my brother broke his leg.
I'm sorry I'm late for school, Miss,
But we couldn't find a peg.
I'm sorry I'm late for school, Miss,
You see, I hurt my head.
I'm sorry I'm late for school, Miss,
My mum didn't get out of bed.
I'm sorry I'm late for school, Miss,
My alarm clock changed time itself.
I'm sorry I'm late for school, Miss,
But I just had no health.

**Lucy Kennedy (8)**
**Dunnottar Primary School, Stonehaven**

## Fear

Fear is black and misty.
The taste of cold air.
It smells of fire and smoke.
I see the leaves flapping this way and that.
It sounds like thunder approaching.
Fear makes me feel scared.

**Oscar Craig (8)**
**Dunnottar Primary School, Stonehaven**

## Wellie Weather

Mist in the mountain days,
Huge big wave days,
Fun for the ducks days,
Wellie weather.

Going to museums days,
Reading a book days,
Staying inside days,
Wellie weather.

Big hurricane days,
River flooding days,
No sun at all days,
Wellie weather.

Everything is soaked days,
Rain is pouring down days,
Very, very muddy days,
Wellie weather.

Running in the puddles days,
Extremely wet days,
African people like the rain days,
Amazing wellie weather!

**Stuart Holley (9)**
**Dunnottar Primary School, Stonehaven**

## Monday's Child

Monday's child is really cuckoo,
Tuesday's child won't flush the loo.
Wednesday's child hogs the bed,
Thursday's child paints everything red.
Friday's child is a naughty child,
Saturday's child isn't very mild
And the child that is born on the seventh day,
Is jolly and noisy and shouts hooray!

**Matthew Ogden (8)**
**Dunnottar Primary School, Stonehaven**

## The Thunderstorm

The wind is like a breath of fire,
The lightning is a blinding light,
The sky is a dark hole,
But put them all together,
It makes a natural disaster.

**Steven Macleod (10)**
**Fallin Primary School, Fallin**

## The Animal Storm

The wind howling like a wolf,
As dark as a panther,
The sound like a lion's roar!
Lightning as fast as a cheetah.

The ground as cold as icy snow
And the animals hear the wind blow.
The horses jump up and down,
As the ground shakes from side to side.

The wind howling like a wolf,
As dark as a panther,
The sound like a lion's roar!
Lightning as fast as a cheetah.

The dark storm fades away
And the dark wolves stop the howling
As the storm ends!

**Billy Irvine (10)**
**Fallin Primary School, Fallin**

## Volcanoes

Smoke coming out like snakes in the sky
As dark as coal
Hot rocks flying out like cannonballs
Burning lava leaks out like egg yolk
Destroying everything in its path
Everybody running like they've never run before
Suddenly, everything goes black.

**Blair Maxwell (10)**
**Fallin Primary School, Fallin**

## Hurricanes

Hurricanes swirl like a spiral,
Howls like a ghost,
As grey as rain clouds,
As fast as a jet.

Demolishing everything in its path,
Debris flying all around,
As people scream like monkeys,
Trying to run away.

Telegraph poles coming out of the ground,
Trees' leaves fly like planes,
Cars getting thrown about with the strong wind.

From space you can see the eye,
All the clouds turning into a spiral,
The clouds go away,
The hurricane has stopped.

**Conor Paterson (10)**
**Fallin Primary School, Fallin**

## Storm!

The wind blows like a lion,
Searching for his prey!
Lightning as bright,
As a sunny day.
Clouds as black as night,
As black as a midnight sky.
Thunder as loud as
Cymbals clashing,
As loud as the
Church bells bashing.

**Erin Perrie (10)**
**Fallin Primary School, Fallin**

## Volcanoes

Lava as runny as egg yolk.
Ash as black as a thousand pens.
Gases as poisonous as a poison powder.
As hot as the sun's beams.

Most of your body, very sweaty.
As terrifying as a nightmare.

Move hometown or city.
Anywhere, but away from here!
Now the town is destroyed.
It's not like a volcanic eruption.
It's like the aftermath of an earthquake.

**Ross McTaggart (10)**
**Fallin Primary School, Fallin**

## Volcano

Smoke coming out like snakes in the sky,
As black as coal and ash.
Smoke coming out like dark chocolate,
Rocks as hot as melting magma.
Burning rocks shooting out of a cannon,
Magma as red as a devil.
Lava spitting out like a pressure washer,
It's like a bomb inside a hole and exploding.

**Liam Kirkwood (10)**
**Fallin Primary School, Fallin**

## Volcano!

Smoke sizzling out,
As foggy as can be,
Filling up the night sky,
Fumes can stay away from me.

Roaring like a lion,
Here comes the lava,
As quick as a cheetah,
As red as red can be.

As hot as flames,
As scary as a tsunami,
As deadly as a dagger,
As evil as murderers.

Time to escape!

**Lauren Smith (10)**
**Fallin Primary School, Fallin**

## Storm!

Wind like a ramming bull,
The rain is as wet as the sea,
Sky is dark as coal,
The lightning looks like a beam of light.

People staying inside,
Not wanting to go out,
There's screaming and shouting everywhere,
There's no way out.

It's raining,
It's thunder and lightning,
It looks like the night,
It's windy as a ship at sea.

**Taylor Reid (10)**
**Fallin Primary School, Fallin**

## Storm

It had wind like a ramming bull,
A beam of light,
Darkness all through,
The storm is like burning fire,
The sky as dark as coal,
All wet puddles everywhere
And lightning struck through the wet doorway.
The rain was like golf balls
Falling from the sky,
But after that the sun was shining from the sky.

**Cheryl Rooney (10)**
**Fallin Primary School, Fallin**

## The Pixies

Down at the bottom of the garden,
Guess what you can see?
Little tiny creatures,
They're quite hard to see.
Little pixies dancing in the summer breeze,
Gorgeous little creatures with wings,
They hide in the mushrooms in your garden grass.

**Natalie Gow (8)**
**Fallin Primary School, Fallin**

## The Black Stallion

The black stallion galloped across the beach,
The sunset came, he gave a tremendous neigh,
No one knew the black stallion was there in the wild,
His mane and tail flew in the wind,
He was gorgeous.

**Karlee Manson (9)**
**Fallin Primary School, Fallin**

## Kittens

K ittens are so cuddly
I sn't it so cute to have a kitten?
T alk to them during the night
T each them to sit without a fright
E at quite a lot, so just nip to the shop
N o fear because the kittens are here
S o loveable and so cute, I love kittens
So should you.

**Leigh Young (9)**
**Fallin Primary School, Fallin**

## Teachers

T eachers, teachers
E very day they come into school
A cting and drawing
C heerful as can be
H ee, hee, hee
E ven when they need to shout
R easonable sometimes
S ometimes mean.

**Alex Govan (9)**
**Fallin Primary School, Fallin**

## The Storm

The wind was fine,
The next minute a tornado was coming on.
The wind was like a ramming bull,
I saw a strike of lightning in the sky.
It is a case of thunder lightning.
The sky was like an ash cloud from a volcano.
There was a crash of rain.
I stood in a puddle, it felt like I was in a swimming pool.

**Lisa Brennan (10)**
**Fallin Primary School, Fallin**

## Love

Love is a pink feeling.
It smells like a fresh spring flower.
It sounds like birds tweeting in the breeze.
It looks like a fluffy world.
It feels like a warm and cuddly feeling.
It tastes like fresh honey.
It reminds me of a magic wonderland.

**Holly Chandler (10)**
**Johnshaven Primary School, Johnshaven**

## Anger

Anger is red, like a fiery dragon
That is really annoyed.
It smells like hot ashes
Spurting out of a volcano.
It feels like something
Is burning in your body.
It tastes hot and spicy.
It sounds like a volcano
Blowing out ashes.
It reminds me of a tree
Blowing fiercely side to side.

**Grant Keith (11)**
**Johnshaven Primary School, Johnshaven**

## Sadness

Sadness is the darkest blue, like the night coming down on the world,
And cold feelings giving you shivers, like a soft wind blowing your
tears away.
It tastes like the salty sea waves crashing slowly into each other.
In your ears there's moaning ghosts waiting for a moment to strike,
With dull, sagging faces, slumping bodies and no love to be shed.
Sadness smells like rotten flowers waiting to be renewed.
Sadness reminds me of an emptiness that is always in my heart
And I will not be right until the end.

**Laura Townsend (9)**
**Johnshaven Primary School, Johnshaven**

## Happiness

Happiness is like a sun
It feels like you're floating in the air as you would never be before
It tastes like good food just sizzling in your mouth
It smells like a flower growing in front
It sounds like birds singing in the trees
It looks like angels floating around me
It reminds me of children and singing and skipping joyfully about.

**Miranda-Beth Leavens (9)**
**Johnshaven Primary School, Johnshaven**

## Love

Love is like a yellow sun beaming in the lovely blue sky.
It looks like two animals running around together.
It smells like the fresh air from the trees and plants.
It feels like two people romantically in love, always together forever.
It tastes like a juicy apple that falls from the sky.
It sounds like birds tweeting and young ones being born.
It reminds me of my mum and dad, always in love!

**Holly Marwick (10)**
**Johnshaven Primary School, Johnshaven**

## Love

Love is like a bunch of pink roses.
Love tastes like strawberries dipped in chocolate.
Love looks like a tree bursting with blossom.
Love smells like chocolate pudding with cream.
Love reminds me of my auntie's wedding in June.

**Lauren Anderson (10)**
**Johnshaven Primary School, Johnshaven**

## Anger

Anger is dark red, like fire
It looks like lava exploding
It makes you feel pain
It tastes like ashes
It smells like hate
It sounds like explosions
It reminds me of a volcano.

**Lewis Pollock (10)**
**Johnshaven Primary School, Johnshaven**

## Love

Love looks like a love heart
Love feels like a soft little kitten
Love tastes like chocolate ice cream
Love sounds like little birds tweeting
Love smells like a red, red rose
Love reminds me of cats, cats, cats, cats,
Cats . . .

**Lisa Porter (7)**
**Johnshaven Primary School, Johnshaven**

## Love

Love is red, like a red, red rose and a red, red heart too.
I love my family as well as you.
It looks like a big, big heart and it sounds like birds singing in
the trees.

Love tastes like strawberry ice cream.
Love feels like a soft, soft puppy.
It reminds me of my mum and dad.

**Kathryn Townsend (6)**
**Johnshaven Primary School, Johnshaven**

## Fear

Fear is scary, cross and bad
Fear is everywhere
Fear is even in the air
It is bad and black
Even in the water.

**Hamish Wright (8)**
**Johnshaven Primary School, Johnshaven**

## Anger

A nger is bad
N ever punch someone
G et into trouble if you do
E very day don't be angry
R ight I am, so *trust* me!

**Dillon Scott (8)**
**Johnshaven Primary School, Johnshaven**

## Anger

Pirates and devils and cowboys and dragons have a lot of anger.
They set off bombs and they create chaos.
Next they cause danger and set cities on fire.
Anger is like an exploding volcano!

**Kyle Boyd (8)**
**Johnshaven Primary School, Johnshaven**

## Love

Love is like a bunch of newly sprung roses.
It tastes like a lovely mint choc chip whippy cone.
It smells like a lavender knitted blanket.
It sounds like waves coming in, scraping on the rocks.
It looks like the sparkling sun winking at you.
It reminds me of paradise.

**Rhys Gardiner (11)**
**Johnshaven Primary School, Johnshaven**

## Sadness

Sadness is blue like rain
Sadness feels like tears
Sadness looks like a dead rabbit
Sadness tastes salty
Sadness sounds like someone crying
Sadness reminds me of my rabbit Lily.

**Murray Dunbar (9)**
**Johnshaven Primary School, Johnshaven**

## Happiness

Pink is the colour for happiness
It tastes like melting chocolate on your tongue
It sounds like children laughing
Happiness looks like a smiling smile
Happiness smells like newly grown blossoms
It reminds me of last summer.

**Stephanie Brannan**
**Johnshaven Primary School, Johnshaven**

## Anger!

Anger is red like a fiery dragon.
It sounds like an explosion.
It looks like a hot bubbling sun.
It smells hot and bitter.
It feels like something blown up inside you.
It tastes bitter!
It reminds me of my dog Buster.

**Tieje Brannan (10)**
**Johnshaven Primary School, Johnshaven**

## A Journey Through The Senses

We can touch the burning food on our plate
And the freezing ice cube in our drink
Some people can't do the same as us

We can taste the refreshing sweet in our mouth
And the hot, spicy food
Some people can't do the same as us

We can smell the smelly feet on a person
And the lovely soapy smell of a person's face
Some people can't do the same as us

We can see the plain piece of paper
And the nice wallpaper in the girl's bedroom
Some people can't do the same as us

We can hear the noisy music next door
And the quiet whisper of a person's voice
Some people can't do the same as us

What I am trying to say is simply -
Senses are amazing!

**Claire McNicoll (11)**
**Juniper Green Primary School, Edinburgh**

## A Journey Through The Senses

We can touch the cold and slippery ice
And the warm air circling us inside
Not everyone can do the same as us

We can taste the sweet taste of honey
And the sour taste of a lemon
Not everyone can do the same as us

We can smell the perfume of the lovely lilies
And the pungent smell of people burning rubbish
Not everyone can do the same as us

We can see tall buildings over the city
And the small eggs getting ready to hatch
Not everyone can do the same as us

We hear the quiet sound of the music playing
And the explosion of a sparkly blue firework
Not everyone can do the same as us

What I am trying to say is -
Not everyone is as lucky as me and you.

**Megan Mackay (10)**
**Juniper Green Primary School, Edinburgh**

## A Journey Through The Senses

I love the feeling of icy cold lemonade as it trickles down your throat,
And the warm feeling of coffee when you take your first sip.
I love senses, how lucky we are to have them!

We can taste the bitter taste of Granny Smith apples when you take
a huge bite,
Also the sweet taste of strawberries with sugar and cream, and
ice cream!
I love senses, how lucky we are to have them!

The smell of fresh lavender when you get really close is
incredibly refreshing,
Just one sniff and you can smell the rotten fish that's been out
for weeks!
I love senses, how lucky we are to have them!

I can see the colourful colours of the rainbow - red, yellow and
much more,
And the dull look of a black and white picture, dusty, just sitting there,
I love senses, how lucky we are to have them!

I like the peaceful sound of a classroom, when the teacher's got the
pupils under control,
But much prefer the noisy sound of a classroom that's not
under control,
I love senses, how lucky we are to have them!

What I'm trying to say is simply -
Senses are amazing, but some people aren't as lucky as us.

**Katie Hill (11)**
**Juniper Green Primary School, Edinburgh**

## A Journey Through The Senses

We can touch the soft, silky fur on a cat
And the brick-hard stone of the pavement.
Some people can't do the same as us.

We can taste the sweet taste of ice cream
And the sour taste of bright yellow lemons.
Some people can't do the same as us.

We can smell the rotten smell of rubbish in a bin
And the lovely smell of fresh strawberries.
Some people can't do the same as us.

We can see the tall trees in the park
And the small bugs in the grass.
Some people can't do the same as us.

We can hear the loud TV turned up full volume
And the quiet sound of mice in the shed.
Some people can't do the same as us.

What I am simply trying to say is . . .
We are better off than we think!

**Bonnie Fisher (10)**
**Juniper Green Primary School, Edinburgh**

## The Five Wonders Of The Body!

The electrifying touch of a TV screen,
Or the soothing feel of a velvet scarf,
What a wonderful sense!

The bland taste of water in a glass
And the flavoursome taste of Italian cuisine,
What a wonderful sense!

The pungent smell of washing up liquid,
The soft smell of newly washed bedding,
What a wonderful sense!

You can see the bright stars at night,
You can also see the dull clouds on a stormy day,
What a wonderful sense!

The calming sound of waves on the still sea,
Or the disturbing sound of screams in the night,
What a wonderful sense!

The exhilarating feel of going to a theme park
And the dampening atmosphere of a funeral,
What a wonderful sense!

I'm very lucky to have all these,
But you might not.

**Murray Drummond (10)**
**Juniper Green Primary School, Edinburgh**

## A Journey Through The Senses

We can touch the soft, spongy surface of a cake
And the sharp, electrifying touch of a TV screen.
Some people can't do the same as us.

We can taste the exploding bitterness of lemons
And the sweet relaxing taste of melting chocolate.
Some people can't do the same as us.

We can smell the hot, soothing smell of coffee
And the cold, refreshing smell of the clean air.
Some people can't do the same as us.

We can see the tall skyscrapers sparkling in the sunlight
And the small, peaceful waves shining on the sea.
Some people can't do the same as us.

We can hear the whispery echo coming through the tunnels
And the loud, disturbing sound of excited football fans.
Some people can't do the same as us.

What I am trying to say is just simply . . .
Some people aren't as lucky as us.

**Shaun Munro (11)**
**Juniper Green Primary School, Edinburgh**

## A Journey Through The Senses

We can touch the cold white snow
And the burning, boiling kettle.
Some of us are very lucky.

We can taste the blasting, sour Starburst
And the strong, salty chips.
Some of us are very lucky.

We can smell the strong, smoky burning
And the sweaty gym hall.
Some of us are very lucky.

We can see the clear, shiny windows
And the dull, cloudy days.
Some of us are very lucky.

We can hear the loud roaring of a lion
And the quiet, soothing classical music.
Some of us are very lucky.

We can feel very full after Christmas dinner
And the hunger before dinner.
Some of us are very lucky.

**Emma Newlands (10)**
**Juniper Green Primary School, Edinburgh**

## My Dog, Alfie

My dog, Alfie,
Is always happy,
Unless he is bad,
He will then look sad.

My dog, Alfie, is sometimes smelly,
He enjoys sitting in front of the telly.

My dog, Alfie, has beautiful eyes,
The annoying thing is he lies down
With numerous sighs.

My dog, Alfie, would eat lots of food,
But we know it is not good.

My dog, Alfie's favourite food is fish,
That he eats in his silver dish.

**Erin Allan (11)**
**Kennethmont School, Huntly**

## My Cat, Archie

My cat, Archie, never lets go,
I walk by him
And with a dash of his paws,
He grabs on my leg
And bites my trousers.
He is like a ninja,
He's very stealthy,
He goes in my sister's bedroom
Full of cuddly toys,
And with a slash of his claws,
Off comes the head of her favourite teddy.
Another slash,
And her toy hammock full of cuddly toys falls,
*Crash!*
Archie's in trouble!

**Daniel Coursey (9)**
**Kennethmont School, Huntly**

## My Dad

Dad, you are the best,
Nothing like the rest.
All the others are boring,
Unlike you who is always snoring.

My dad is not bad,
But he is sometimes sad.
He is always up early,
Harvesting the barley.

Then it is time for lambing,
Now he has a bad aroma.
I like to help on the farm,
My dad has a great charm.

My dad likes his lunch,
He goes *munch, munch.*
He also likes his supper,
Including a cup of tea.
Then it's time for his bed.

**Peter Duthie (11)**
**Kennethmont School, Huntly**

## Football

F ootball is fun
O ver and
O ver the ball rolls
T hrough the net and on the road
B other! He ran past me
A nd now he is shooting
L aughing at him missing
L ying on the ground, killing myself laughing.

**Kyle Florence (10)**
**Kennethmont School, Huntly**

## My Dog, Molly

My dog's called Molly,
She is always very jolly.
We call her Moll,
She is pretty small,
Compared to Meig,
Who steals washing pegs.
Moll likes meat,
She's very neat.
She has a tail that curls,
It also unfurls.
Her favourite walk is New Hills,
Best thing is I don't have to pay bills.
She chases rabbits,
But she hates carrots.
She used to eat Weetabix and milk,
Her coat is like silk.
She has twenty claws,
She likes to chase jackdaws.
She lies near the fire,
Much to her desire.
As I watch the telly,
I rub her belly.
Now she will relax,
With her coat as warm as wax.

**Angus MacLean (11)**
**Kennethmont School, Huntly**

## My Cat, Kelly

I have a cat,
But she's not really fat.
Her name is Kelly,
She's not at all smelly.
She does what she likes,
But never ever bites.
She is the colour cream,
She also makes me sneeze.
She doesn't like the loft,
But her fur is incredibly soft.
She hates outdoors,
And prefers laminate floors.
My dad I miss,
So I give her a kiss.
I put down my mug,
When she wants a hug.
She likes playing with laces,
In lots of different places.
She has a brother, Jack,
And he is quite fat.
They are both four years old
And they never get cold.
I love Kelly heaps
And she's mine for keeps.

**Morgan McCallum (11)**
**Kennethmont School, Huntly**

## My Cat Called Ten

My fat cat is called Ten,
She moves as slow as a slug,
Except when she is chased.
My cat loves gammon,
She sleeps like a baby on her cushion.
When she moves her right leg forward,
Her tummy moves to the left.
Her tail is long,
Her tail is fluffy,
Her tail is puffy.
She may bite and scratch,
But only if you push her off the bed.
I feed her in the morning,
We feed her whenever she paws her bowl.
My family sometimes call her Old Took.

**Matthew Robertson (10)**
**Kennethmont School, Huntly**

## Balls

Bouncing balls,
All around,
Lift them up,
Let them down,
Watch them go up and down.
Bouncing balls,
All around.

Bouncing balls,
Make a sound,
Some are soft,
Some are hard.
Balls for different sports,
Bouncing balls,
Make a sound.

Bouncing balls,
Hit the ground,
Kick them high,
Kick them hard.
Footballs are my favourite ball,
Bouncing balls,
All around.

**Cara Simpson (11)**
**Kennethmont School, Huntly**

## My Big Sister

I am ten years old,
My sis is thirteen years old.
She is very brave and bold,
But I still hate my big sis.

I hit my big sis,
She tries to hit me,
But it's a big miss.

My sis snores at night
And I can give her such a fright.
She also likes sweets and treats
And that's my big sis
*Jacqueline!*

**Rebekah Watson (10)**
**Kennethmont School, Huntly**

## What Has Happened To The World?

The ice is melting,
The seasons have changed,
The Earth is disappearing,
It has been completely rearranged.
Reduce, reuse, recycle,
And help as much as you can,
Stop using lots of chemicals,
To save the species of man.
Walk to school,
Switch off the light,
Don't watch too much TV,
Make the Earth feel right!
We don't want snow in May,
We don't want frost in June,
We all have a part to play,
Otherwise the Earth will vanish soon.

**Stephanie Curtis (11)**
**Kirkmichael Primary School, Blairgowrie**

## A Couple Of Cats

I have a couple of cats
One is very fat and the other is quite black.
They are both girls
And love my pearls.
When I touch their fur,
They like to purr.
When they have fleas,
They chase the bees.
And now you've heard
All you can hear,
I'll go grab
A pint of beer!

**Fiona Van Der Veldt (11)**
**Kirkmichael Primary School, Blairgowrie**

## My Rabbits

My rabbits are so funny,
They are my bunnies
And they are so crawly
All night and day.
They are so cute
And they love eating fruit.
They love to hop and bop
All night and all day.

**Aarron Laidler (10)**
**Kirkmichael Primary School, Blairgowrie**

## This Old Beardy

There's this old beardy, he's really old and hairy,
He likes to run and tumble, but he always ends up in a bundle.
He eats a lot of grub and he is a great bit dug.
He's really cute and sometimes covered in soot.
His name is Joy and he loves his toy.

**Holly Brown (10)**
**Kirkmichael Primary School, Blairgowrie**

## My Dog, Mr Wendal

I have a dog called Mr Wendal
He loves to chase his toy
Yes, and before you ask, he is a boy
I love my dog
He eats like a hog
But is not very fat
He's got a big furry mat
But he is the best dog
In the whole world.

**Frankie Moore (10)**
**Kirkmichael Primary School, Blairgowrie**

## The Bumping Car

The bumping car
Goes *ra, ra, ra,*
As it goes down the street.
When it goes by,
We always say hi,
But the posh people say, *oh my!*
The bumping car,
Is red and shiny,
You will never see it,
Dirty and grimy.
It stays in a small garage
And is no way as elegant
As a horse and carriage.

**Claire Van Der Veldt (10)**
**Kirkmichael Primary School, Blairgowrie**

## I Have A Pet Monkey!

I have a pet monkey,
Her name is Funky.
She only drinks beer,
She has no fear.
Her favourite food is pie,
That's something no one can deny.
She is twelve years old,
She says she's never cold.
She's always fighting with Crystal,
That's my cat who's very mystical.
Funky jumps around,
You can hear her a million miles away with that sound.
She lives in my greenhouse,
With an unexpected mouse.
The greenhouse is full of plants,
There's even a platform for her to dance.
The greenhouse roof is a dome
And she said she feels right at home!

**Annie Winton (11)**
**Kirkmichael Primary School, Blairgowrie**

## Anger

Anger is the colour red, like danger.
Anger is the sound of thunder roaring.
Anger is the smell of out of date milk.
Anger is the taste of nothing.
Anger feels like frustration.
It reminds me of my dad.

**Ross Ferguson (12)**
**Knoxland Primary School, Dumbarton**

## Anger

Anger is the colour red,
Like the raging fans at Stamford Bridge.
Anger is the sound of exploding bombs
In Iraq.
Anger is the taste of revenge,
When the defenceless man got attacked by a youth.
Anger is the touch of a kidnapper
In Portugal.
Anger reminds me of
A narrow-minded bigot.

**Alexander Brown (12)**
**Knoxland Primary School, Dumbarton**

## Darkness

Darkness is the colour black, like a deep black cave.
Darkness is the sound of an owl tooting in the forest.
Darkness is the taste of my mum's horrible mince pies.
Darkness is the smell of falling down a dark hole.
Darkness is the look of my large, empty bedroom in the middle
of the night.
Darkness is the feel of a black spot hitting your face.
Darkness reminds me of a very dark night in the street.

**Jordan Brooks (11)**
**Knoxland Primary School, Dumbarton**

## Darkness

Darkness is like the starless sky,
With no moon to guide you.
Darkness is like the colour black,
With all the brightness gone eternally.
Darkness is like the sound of leaking pipes,
With the echo reverberating around the room.
Darkness is like the taste of $H^2O$,
With no taste at all to sense.
Darkness is like the smell of standing water,
With the muck adding a slight acridity.
Darkness is like the sight of a massacre's aftermath,
With no one alive to heed your calls.
Darkness is like the feel of empty space,
With no one or nothing at all.
Darkness is like the memories of someone's passing,
With the whole world seeming to plunge into darkness.
Darkness is the black oblivion,
Where all things seem to disappear.

**Mark Provan (11)**
**Knoxland Primary School, Dumbarton**

## Fun

Fun is the colour of yellow,
Like the hot summer sun - great to play in all day.
Fun is the sound of laughter,
People running around having loads of fun.
Fun tastes like vanilla-iced birthday cake,
Amusement and entertainment all in the back garden.
Balloons and streamers are good!
Fun smells like cakes, sweets, fast food and ice cream,
Eating them all day long.
Fun looks like . . . well, fun!
Games, food, *cooool* drinks and staying up late! It's great!
Fun feels great, I love it!
The wind in my hair, the warmth of the sunset,
But it's not all good when the midges come out! *Oooooooh!*

All the descriptions of fun remind of when I was three;
Everything was a great big adventure. Then best fun ever!

**Liam Troup (12)**
**Knoxland Primary School, Dumbarton**

## Sectarianism

S adness caused by hurtful chants
E nergetic punches going through my face
C rowd screaming for their team
T errified to go to old firm matches because of fights
A lways running from sectarianism
R espect me, I'm like everybody else
I nside I'm the same as you, forget about my religion
*Or what team I support . . .*
A fter matches, fear of getting in a fight
N o reason for all the hate
I gnore it, I've been told
S ectarianism
M ourning, people getting killed in fights of religion or
What team you support . . .

*Don't sit back and watch sectarianism*
*Help stamp it out . . .*
*Think!*

**Isla Neil (12)**
**Knoxland Primary School, Dumbarton**

## Anti-Sectarianism

S ectarianism is appalling. It really has to stop!
E xcitement ruined by horrible chanting.
The game gets spoilt because of the fighting.
C onfused and distressed because of all these parades.
T rying to ignore it, but it just won't stop.
A ll the fighting and horrible chanting, makes me really scared.
R angers fans are chanting horrible things to the Celtic fans,
And I am terrified.
I 'm trying not to think about all the victims
That have been killed because of sectarianism.
A lso fights about religion, that is just as scary.
N obody cares about the people getting killed,
Which I think is absolutely disgraceful.
I gnore it is what I try to do, but it is very hard.
S ectarianism has to stop, it is very horrible, so let's make it stop.
M y wish has not come true,
Sectarianism has not stopped, hopefully it will soon.

**Ashlinn Weber (11)**
**Knoxland Primary School, Dumbarton**

## Sectarianism

Sectarianism is all around me,
Separation puts me in despair,
I can't escape it,
People shouting, screaming,
It makes me die inside,
It just doesn't stop there,
Every day is the same,
It happens everywhere I go.
I'm in misery,
The police are here trying to break it up,
No matter what, nothing will ever cheer me up
And now after this torture,
I'm dead inside because of this terrible pain.
Every day is always the same,
Cruelty and abuse.
To me it's just old news,
*Sectarianism needs to end!*

**Laura Fleming (12)**
**Knoxland Primary School, Dumbarton**

## Sectarianism Is . . .

S houting and bawling for a pointless score
E nding in unreasonable fights and brawls
C eltic - it's only a name on a top
T he clash of religion
A ppalling songs with nasty words
R acism is exactly the same
I gnore it all you can, but at some point you will snap
A gain and again the abuse gets louder and nastier
N ow I feel ashamed all these fights are caused by religion
I gnore it, nobody is better than you, we are all different
S ectarianism - all it is is bullying
M ake it stop *now!*

**Rebecca Bell (11)**
**Knoxland Primary School, Dumbarton**

# Hate

Hate is red and orange, like molten lava.
Hate sounds like a volcano erupting.
Hate tastes like biting into a sour grape.
Hate smells like a building bombed by terrorists.
Hate sounds like two people arguing.
Hate feels like a lion roaring in your chest.
Hate reminds me of all the wars.

**Stephen Bennett (11)**
**Knoxland Primary School, Dumbarton**

## Fun

Fun is blue, like a cloudless sky.
Fun sounds like children laughing at the fair.
Fun tastes like chocolate dribbling down your throat.
Fun smells like hot chocolate sitting in a cup.
Fun looks like children playing games in a field.
Fun feels like my dog's fur rubbing against my hand.
Fun is when you go somewhere you really like.
Fun is when you're doing something that makes you happy.

**Sean Deeney (11)**
**Knoxland Primary School, Dumbarton**

## Love

Love is like a deep passion,
As deep as the happiness in my heart.
Love is crimson,
As crimson as a blazing fire which burns away the pain.
Love tastes so sweet,
As sweet as the icing on a freshly baked cake.
Love reminds me of a lot of things,
Things that I love,
People that I love,
Everything that I love.

**Jenna Wilson (11)**
**Knoxland Primary School, Dumbarton**

## Love

Love is the colour rose, like a flower on a hot summer's day.
Love sounds like a harp playing a romantic tune.
Love tastes sweet like sugar and strong like honey.
Love smells like running through a field of roses.
Love looks like a balloon that you're too scared to let go of.
Love feels like a fluffy pink pillow you hold every night.
Love reminds me of my family and friends that I adore so much.

**Gemma Kitchen (11)**
**Knoxland Primary School, Dumbarton**

## Fun

Fun is the colour of the blazing, blue sky.
Fun sounds like a race car zooming by.
Fun tastes like sugary candyfloss melting in my mouth.
Fun smells like toffee popcorn rising in the air.
Fun looks like a speeding roller coaster on its tracks.
Fun feels like having an excellent time with my friends.
Fun reminds me of the first day I played football.

**Becky Fisher (11)**
**Knoxland Primary School, Dumbarton**

## Darkness

Darkness is a starless winter night,
Funerals, tears of gloom, tears of despair.
Darkness is black and the sound of silence,
The smell of a sombre way of life.
The looks of the darkness, the unlit light.
Shadows take over a life, maybe one of yours.

**Scott Dallas (11)**
**Knoxland Primary School, Dumbarton**

## Darkness

Darkness is the oldest tree that crackles in the mist.
Darkness is the poverty that surely can't be missed.
With all the children in Africa, there may be some hope there,
But then the life that we lead surely can't compare.
Darkness is that dirty water, which they have to drink,
It causes so many illnesses of which they do not think.
Darkness feels like there's no hope
And I don't know how the Africans can cope.
Darkness smells like gunfire by men
And most African children die before the age of ten.
Darkness makes me think how lucky I am
And when I grow older, I will give what I can.

**Jordan MacLean (11)**
**Knoxland Primary School, Dumbarton**

## Love

Love is the colour red, like the colour of roses.
Love is the sound of children having fun.
Love tastes like chocolate and it smells like flowers.
Love is in the form of a heart and feels as soft as silk,
But the best thing about love is it reminds me of my family.

**Calum Harper (11)**
**Knoxland Primary School, Dumbarton**

## Happiness

Happiness is black and white, like kicking racism out.
It sounds jubilant and sends me into raptures.
Happiness tastes like melted cheese on nachos.
To me happiness looks like everyone being friends and no
more bigotry.
It makes me feel warm and helps my heart beat more smoothly.
It reminds me of moments I had with my family,
Even the ones who are no longer here.

**Scott Connie (12)**
**Knoxland Primary School, Dumbarton**

## Silence . . .

Silence is white, like an empty room, like nothing.
Silence is the sound of no news, but anticipating the worst.
Silence is the taste of water, so bland and clear.
Silence is the smell of emptiness, like loneliness, like non-existence.
Silence is sadness, seeing lips move guessing what you have to say.
Silence is tiresome.
Silence is troublesome.
Silence . . .

**Gillian McElroy (12)**
**Knoxland Primary School, Dumbarton**

## Hate

Hate is the colour of black and white, like racism.
Hate is the sound of people in the streets fighting.
Hate tastes like just after you have dry swallowed a pill.
Hate looks like my mum when she gets out of bed in the morning.
Hate feels like two-faced people stabbing me in the back
with swords.
Hate reminds me of all the intolerable sectarianism and racism
in the world.

**Stacey O'Hara (12)**
**Knoxland Primary School, Dumbarton**

## Happiness

Happiness, happiness, happiness is green
Just like all the plants in spring all around the field
Happiness, happiness, sounds like laughter from a thousand people
Happiness, happiness, tastes like an orange, sweet and refreshing
Happiness, happiness, looks like a rainbow, all the colours in the sky
Happiness, happiness, reminds me of the summer when we play until it's dark.

**Ruaraidh MacGregor (11)**
**Knoxland Primary School, Dumbarton**

## Hunger

Hunger is the colour of white,
like it is empty.
Hunger is the sound of clattering,
like plates coming out of the cupboard.
Hunger is the taste of nothing
as you are hungry.
Hunger is the smell of food
as you are desperate for it.
Hunger feels like pain
like you have a sore stomach.
Hunger reminds me of a restaurant
waiting to be served.

**Andrew McKenzie (12)**
**Knoxland Primary School, Dumbarton**

## Stop

Stop sectarianism,
Stop the fight,
Stop the arguing,
Stop the misery.
Just stop it all.
Let's get together,
For peace begins with us.
For it's affecting us,
Me, you, your family.
It's affecting people,
I don't know why.
It will be better to team up,
Stop being awful,
Before it's the sorrow.
The fighting, it drives me mad,
With people's harsh words,
We just give up.
Please, let's bring peace.

**Rebecca Law (11)**
**Knoxland Primary School, Dumbarton**

## Sectarianism

S tupid and worthless
E very word is hurtful
C reating trouble wherever it goes
T errible cruelty
A round religion and football
R iots break out
I see no point in it
A ppalling songs and chants
N o reason for it
I ntimidating every victim
S elfish people abusing others
M y opinion of sectarianism.

**Graeme Burt (11)**
**Knoxland Primary School, Dumbarton**

## Sectarianism

Sectarianism is horrific,
We should be ashamed,
Some people think it's terrific,
But it makes me want to scream.

Rangers and Celtic are
Sometimes a nightmare,
It's completely appalling,
People take it too far,
Like Catholic and Protestants.

Sectarianism has to stop,
It is such a terrible thing,
If we stop it now,
There will be no more pointless fights again.

**Kirsty Harrison (12)**
**Knoxland Primary School, Dumbarton**

## Anti-Sectarianism

S top sectarianism, it's very bigoted
I feel very disappointed that people do it
E xtinguish sectarianism, put it out,
Hear the call of people shout
C ongratulations to the winning team
You don't need to fight about it
T ry and try for people to stop it
If you don't Scotland will be ruined
A stonished by the childish behaviour
One by one they talk about each other
R ebellious, they think they are
Not letting them work for you
I ntimidated by the awful chanting
People shouting shocking words
A ppalling things that people say
You Protestant, you Catholic
N ever quite at an old firm
The winning team gets the most shouts
I gnore it the police say
How can you when you're getting threatened?
S houting for their favourite team
Are they shouting because of their religion?
M eaningless, this sectarianism
Songs, lyrics, will this ever stop?

**Konal Lee (11)**
**Knoxland Primary School, Dumbarton**

## Anti-Sectarianism Poem

Sectarianism, it's everywhere,
At football matches,
Songs and chants I've never heard,
So offensive, so horrific,
I wish it would stop,
Yesterday I went for a job interview,
Questions not normal,
About my religion,
Disgraceful,
Awful,
I wish it would stop,
Last week I went to Northern Ireland,
Scary, scary, scary!
The kerbstone different colours,
These guys are mental,
These guys are crazy,
I wish it would stop,
Last month I was walking to Global,
Wearing a Celtic top,
The Orange March went by,
I got jeered and punched,
I was lying on the ground,
Beaten, scared.
*Sectarianism -*
*Think about it!*

**Craig Runciman (12)**
**Knoxland Primary School, Dumbarton**

## Anti-Sectarianism

Sectarianism, sectarianism,
Oh, how I am confused,
If I saw a sectarian person,
I would not take my hat off to them.

Horror at the football park,
I look around in shame,
Hearing boos and chants all around,
I don't see why people do this horrible thing.

We all have two eyes,
Two ears,
Two arms,
Two legs,
One nose
And one mouth.
We all have different personalities.
So let's stop *now!*
*Think about it!*

**Shannon Smith (12)**
**Knoxland Primary School, Dumbarton**

## Sectarianism

S tand up to sectarianism, don't sit back, fight back
E xplosive thoughts and feelings
C eltic and Rangers must stop fighting
T errified one day you might be the victim
A ngry about all the people getting hurt
R acism is the equivalent of sectarianism
I gnoring it will only make it worse, so stand up
A ppalling the names that they call each other
N ot acceptable because there is no need
I gnorant they are because of the way they treat each other
S ectarianism
M ust stop *now!*

**Jade Smith (11)**
**Knoxland Primary School, Dumbarton**

## Sectarianism

S ectarianism should stop! It is despicable.
E veryone fighting!
Screams and cries for help, it is horrible
I can't stand it anymore, I wish it was gone!
C utting up sectarianism I am trying
But whatever I do it won't stop it!
T rying to ignore it all, but I can't' it is too horrible,
I guess my wish has not come true and it never will
A wful, it is awful.
R ound and round sectarianism goes, like a whirlpool of horror.
I nto the football stadium I go, Rangers beat Celtic
Fans beating up police.
'It's only a game,' I shout, but no one listens.
A nimals, they are acting like animals.
*No,* animals behave better than them!
N o one cares about sectarianism!
I gnore it, I will try.
S ectarianism,
M ust stop!

**Scott Major (11)**
**Knoxland Primary School, Dumbarton**

## Anti-Sectarianism

S ectarianism must stop! It makes me so angry and disgusted.
E xcitement spoiled by songs and chanting. All the fighting
ruins the fun.
C onfused and distressed by the appalling parade,
disappointed and ashamed.
T ry to ignore it, but it won't go away!
A ll the horrific name calling and changing causes great discomfort.
R angers and Celtic, they're only football teams,
no fighting was meant.
I ntimidation caused for no reason.
A ppalling and pointless, it should not happen!
N ot wanted or needed.
I hate it!
S ectarianism
*M ust stop!*

**David McCaffary (11)**
**Knoxland Primary School, Dumbarton**

## Anti-Sectarianism

Excuses, just excuses,
How does anyone rip someone to shreds?
Football matches, schools or other countries,
It doesn't matter.
A minority of bigots,
Not allowing people to be different.
Varieties of a religion not allowed to be shown.
Disgusting comments, intimidating everyone.
Nearly everyone thinks this is wrong,
They believe sectarianism is a social barrier.
Protestant, Catholic, Shi'ite, Sunni,
Glasgow to Baghdad, religion shouldn't separate.
Countries have lost pride in themselves,
Causing anger and hatred.
Creating war,
Driving them into a dead end . . .
There is hope,
We can fight back,
Not by punching, but by protesting non violently.
There must be an end to sectarianism and it ends *now!*

**Jordan Ferguson (12)**
**Knoxland Primary School, Dumbarton**

## Sectarianism Poem

Rangers and Celtic fans chanting horrific sounds,
Trying to scream to make them stop,
Football players are disgusted,
Stop!
Horrified about all the fans,
Not wanting to hear anymore,
Trying to get out,
Stop!
Terrified with people fighting around me,
I think it's not acceptable,
I think Catholic and Protestant are the same,
Stop!

**Rebecca Lyall (12)**
**Knoxland Primary School, Dumbarton**

## Sectarianism Poem

Sectarianism drives me round the bend
The sound of chanting
How can they put up with it?
It would make me faint
The only time the idiots are quiet
Is when a goal is in sight.
It's not just football that gets me going
But the people who can't accept your religion.
The man at market not going to serve
But why?
Catholic and Protestant, what's the difference?
I want it to stop, do you?

**Callum MacLeod (11)**
**Knoxland Primary School, Dumbarton**

## I Am Different

I am different
I am grey
And everyone else
They are in colour.
It is as if
There is a
Crowd of
People laughing
At me.
No matter
How much
I run
They are almost
Queuing up
To do this.
I cannot
Sleep at night
Because
Of this
Problem.
I can't
Imagine
What it is
Like to not
Have this problem.

**Calum Donaghy (11)**
**Knoxland Primary School, Dumbarton**

## Love

Love is the colour yellow because it's bright and cheery.
Love is the sound of people talking and sharing feelings,
Working and playing together like best friends should.
Love is the smell of langneya, like it's all running down your throat.
Love is the look of the sunshine shining on the seabed.
Love is the feeling of a melted chocolate bar.
*Just think how lucky we are.*

**Iain Allen (11)**
**Knoxland Primary School, Dumbarton**

## Lilies

Lilies are pretty and might be
Stingy, but they smell good in spring.
Lilies come in two different colours,
Red and yellow, maybe even blue.
Lilies look great after they blossom
So if you see one, I hope you will jump
Up and shout *wow!*

**Chloe Randall (8)**
**Longforgan Primary School, Longforgan**

## Sport

S port is fun to do
P lay football and have some fun
O n Monday they play the FA final
R un and play as best you can
T here are lots of people playing football with you.

**Holly Hutchison (7)**
**Longforgan Primary School, Longforgan**

## My Friends

My friends are nice,
They are kind too,
I play with them a lot,
They are cool too,
I like their sports and all of their stuff.

We stick together and it is fun.
Having fun with all my friends.
After school we play every day.

We never fall out.
I listen to the birds singing.
I always think I know that song.

**Beth McNeish (7)**
**Longforgan Primary School, Longforgan**

## Sport

S port is healthy for you
P layers play football, they are good
O n Saturday they sometimes play football
R un, jump and kick
T ennis is a great sport too
It's my favourite sport.

**Robyn McNally (7)**
**Longforgan Primary School, Longforgan**

## My Favourite Things

Doggies, butterflies and loads of other things.
I love them so much, I would play with them all day.
The butterflies that I see, they are so colourful and beautiful.
Parties are my favourite things as well,
Because you get birthday cake.
Now that's all my favourite things.

**Lucy Stewart (8)**
**Longforgan Primary School, Longforgan**

## My Best Brother

M y brother is Gavin
Y ou are the best, Gavin

B est brother for life
E verywhere my brother is there
S port, let's play sport
T o play with Gavin is great

B est playing ever
R yan and Gavin
O n Sunday we play on the trampoline
T he Gavin I know is strong
H e is the best
E verywhere we are together
R yan and Gavin are brothers.

**Ryan Anderson (8)**
**Longforgan Primary School, Longforgan**

## About Me

K ieran is the best
I am mad about football
E xcellent at some stuff
R ubbish at some stuff
A dam, Ben A and David are my best friends
N uts about Dundee United

F antastic!

**Kieran Fitzgerald (8)**
**Longforgan Primary School, Longforgan**

## About My Friends

My friends are so nice
They are so kind and we always play together.
We never fall out with each other
At things we're stuck on.
One of them is called Bruce
And he is really clever.
That's one of my friends.
There are another two who act like monkeys
And they are called Murphy and Jamie.
There is another boy who thinks he is really cool.

**Ryan Lonie (8)**
**Longforgan Primary School, Longforgan**

## What I Love

Parties, presents, PlayStation, sweets,
TV, holidays, McFly and treats.
Lying in the sun when the birds are singing,
A hug from my dad and a kiss from my mum.
Having fun with my friends all day,
Robot Wars, sleeping over and shouting hooray!
These are the things that I love.

**Heather Morgans (8)**
**Longforgan Primary School, Longforgan**

## Sport

S port is the best
P layers come from lots of teams
O n Sunday they play football
R un and jump, throw and catch
T here are lots of teams.

**Bruce Kerr (8)**
**Longforgan Primary School, Longforgan**

## Chocolate

C hocolate is nice
H aving lots of chocolate
O h, it is so nice
C ocoa beans make chocolate
O h, it is so, so yum
L ovely chocolate
A whole chocolate bar
T ime to eat chocolate
E very day I eat chocolate, every day.

**Lauren Hutton (9)**
**Longforgan Primary School, Longforgan**

## Fish

F ish is yummy
I like salmon
S almon is a type of fish
H addock is good.

**Murray Macdonald (8)**
**Longforgan Primary School, Longforgan**

## Horses Are Fab

H orses jump, run and gallop
O ver and over again
R aces are fun to watch
S port they do to train for you
E verywhere I go, horses will be there
S port they need to do races

A nd I want to go to a jump show
R un in races, lots of fun
E verywhere I'll see horses, I like to see them jump

F orever horses are there
A ll the time I'll see them there
B eautiful horses are the best.

**Rebecca Strachan (8)**
**Longforgan Primary School, Longforgan**

## The Best Books

'Little Women',
A good book for all
And it doesn't have pictures,
No, none at all.

'The Shrunken Head',
A very scary book
And you must be courageous,
If you dare to take a look.

'The Cat Mummy',
A very sad book, you see,
Because the cat dies,
Prepared you must be.

'The Wizard Of Oz',
The characters are good,
The Tin Man, The Lion
And The Scarecrow made of wood.

**Tori Grigg (9)**
**Wardie Primary School, Edinburgh**

## The Tall Tree

As long as a skipping rope
Growing under the ground,
Going down and twirling round.

As rough as a pineapple
Picked off a tree,
As tall as a giraffe standing with me.

As thick as a brick,
As long as a rope,
This tree is a very old oak.

As green as the grass,
As light as a feather,
As smooth as plastic and as cold as the weather.

**Samantha Fyfe (9)**
**Wardie Primary School, Edinburgh**

## A Tree In The Summer

Twisting and turning underground,
Faster they grow, don't make a sound.

Its thin branches, so long and royal,
How they turn and feel so free.

How the colourful waterfall falls,
They feel so determined to get away
From the glorious tree.

How far it grows does not stop,
Who knows when it will halt at a stop,
It grows as quick as a hare running in a race.

**Paul Macrae (10)**
**Wardie Primary School, Edinburgh**

## Seasons

S pring is . . .
P ansies
R abbits and deer
I n the lovely bright sun
N o one can stop them coming out
G oodies and treats for Easter, yum.

A utumn is . . .
U nbelievably
T empting and fun
U nder the sun
M ore leaves keep falling off
N oon is so dark, I can't see.

S ummer is . . .
U nmistakably hot
M ore sun and
M ore sun
E lephants will enjoy the sun
R ound at the zoo.

W inter is . . .
I n very cold weather
N ever, never be bad because
T omorrow Santa comes round and you have
E ven more presents
R ound the seasons go like a merry-go-round.

**Joe Newman (9)**
**Wardie Primary School, Edinburgh**

## The Growing Tree

Starts from the bottom,
Grows to the top,
On and on,
Will this tree ever stop?

As it grows,
The branches follow,
This tree is,
Very hollow!

Starts small,
Feeds the tree,
These roots
Are as grubby as me!

Getting greener,
Every day,
The leaves,
Are colourful in May.

**James Tait (9)**
**Wardie Primary School, Edinburgh**

## The Four Fab Seasons

Winter is cold, frosty and freezy,
Wind in the winter is breezy,
You can make snowmen so round, fat and jolly
And then cover them with holly.

Spring is nice,
You can see baby mice,
Poke down their holes
And you might find some moles.

Summer is fun
You can bathe in the sun,
Go in the pool
And have some fun.

Autumn is fun,
You can crunch in the leaves,
Fall in leaves
Right up to your knees.

**Rory McDermid (10)**
**Wardie Primary School, Edinburgh**

## A Small Tree

As green as grass,
All big and small,
As thin as pancakes, but most of all?

Digging deep,
So big and small,
But baby ones aren't as tall as all.

As brown as a chocolate bar,
As long as a giraffe's neck,
It makes me feel cool from the sun.

As rough as a rock,
As cracked as shells,
It makes me feel happy.

**Kaitlin Maloney (9)**
**Wardie Primary School, Edinburgh**

## The Fabulous Four Seasons

Spring is a whole new year,
When chicks are born and disappear,
Flowers grow from day to night
And need lots of bright light.

Summer is here, everyone can cheer,
This is the season that makes people pleasing.
Fun and laughter round and round,
People eating ice creams out of bounds.

When autumn comes everyone hums,
Everyone's dull, but the leaves are not very dull at all.
When people go out to play, there is nothing there,
Apart from a big bunch of leaves.
People scrunch them up and make little beads.

When winter comes people snuggle up,
Waiting for bed like a big cosy bear.
Who knows if snow will come, if it does,
Give us some gloves.
Making snowmen is a very hard job,
Getting cold and very old.

**Ryan Crombie (10)**
**Wardie Primary School, Edinburgh**

## Super Seasons

Spring is like a rabbit,
So springy and bright,
It will keep on springing
All through the day and night.

Winter is like ice, oh so cool,
Winter is fun for everyone!
After Father Christmas comes knocking,
You can look in your stocking.

Autumn is fun when you play in the trees
With the falling leaves.

Summer is hot, like an oven,
Summer melts everyone!
If you really want a tan,
Don't stay in your van.

**Lynsey Wilson (9)**
**Wardie Primary School, Edinburgh**

## The Seasons

Spring is fab,
The grass is as green
As a green jumper,
People roll eggs down hills.

Summer is scorching,
At the beach you've got
Sun, sea and sand,
Also enjoy the garden with me.

Autumn is cool,
The wind is whistling past you,
As fast as lightning.
Leaves fall off the trees,
With so many colours.

Winter is the best,
Presents and all,
The snow is as white,
As a fluffy rug.

**Ben Paterson (9)**
**Wardie Primary School, Edinburgh**

## The Most Majestic Tree Of The Forest

The king of the forest
Majestic is he
High above the forest canopy
Arms out in a greeting as if to say
*What are you doing, why go this way?*

Standing high in all his glory
He's had a long life and has lots of stories
Surrounded by a carpet of shining white snowdrops
Rain from the trees looks like wet teardrops.

Withered, old branches as old as the ages
Has the majestic tree as wise as the sages.

The most majestic tree of the forest
The most majestic is he
This is the story
Of the great tree.

**Evan Adair (10)**
**Wardie Primary School, Edinburgh**

## The Four Seasons

As green as the grass,
It makes your heart pound,
All of the lambs
Are running around!

I'm sitting in the paddling pool,
My feet are in the water,
I'm licking at an ice cream,
But the weather's getting hotter!

As dark as a rain cloud,
Hovering above,
It is quite cold just now,
So everybody's wearing gloves!

Christmas is coming,
The geese are getting fat,
I'm receiving lots of presents,
Including a woolly hat!

**Caitriona Campbell (10) & Justyna Kazmeerzack (11)**
**Wardie Primary School, Edinburgh**

## The Growing Tree

Starts from the bottom,
Grows to the top,
On and on,
Will it ever stop?

As it grows,
The branches follow,
This tree is
Very hollow.

Starts small,
Feeds the tree,
These roots
Are as grubby as me.

Getting greener,
Every day,
The leaves are colourful,
In May.

**Morgan Ormiston (9)**
**Wardie Primary School, Edinburgh**

## Seasons

Winter of course Santa comes
He brings presents and toys for the little ones
He's happy, he's jolly
He hates the sun, but he's so much fun.

Spring of course, Easter comes
Flowers are strong, daisies are strong
But the bunny always comes along.

Summer of course, the sun comes, it's hot
It's boiling, it's definitely summer
But when it goes it's such a bummer.

Autumn of course, I don't really like it that much
It's really boring as such.

I hope you enjoyed this poem
I hope you thought it was fun
But it's actually done.

**Andrew Gray (10)**
**Wardie Primary School, Edinburgh**

## What I Like About The Seasons

W inter is fun
I like the snow-white and cold
N atural animals come out at night to play
T ime to open your presents now it's Xmas Day
E veryone is happy now that they have more toys
R ain, rain on the snow, melt and melt all day long

S ummer is hot, summer is cool, everyone has their paddling pool
U nder the slide where people hide from the sun
M ummies and daddies are here to help make sure suncream's on
M um is making the bbq while Dad gets the paddling pool
E arly in the morning the sun rises
R ainbow is shining over the town

S pring is sunny, lovely and warm
P eople are happy catching the butterflies
R ustling branches and new baby lamb just born
I n the zoo a koala has arrived just a day ago
N ear the shop there are flowers just sprouted
G irls and boys play with the conkers

A utumn is a time people are happy
U nder the pile of leaves out comes the children
T ime to have some fun, jump in the leaves
U nderage babies are smiling at the falling leaves
M any people are catching the leaves from the tree
N aughty children are diving in the leaves getting muddy.

**Mia Harley (9)**
**Wardie Primary School, Edinburgh**

# Young Writers Information

We hope you have enjoyed reading this book - and that you will continue to enjoy it in the coming years.

If you like reading and writing poetry drop us a line, or give us a call, and we'll send you a free information pack.

Alternatively if you would like to order further copies of this book or any of our other titles, then please give us a call or log onto our website at www.youngwriters.co.uk

**Young Writers Information**
**Remus House**
**Coltsfoot Drive**
**Peterborough**
**PE2 9JX**

**(01733) 890066**